Teach Me...™
Everyday
HEBREW
Volume 1

Written by Judy Mahoney
Illustrated by Patrick Girouard

Technology is changing our world. Far away exotic places have literally become neighbors.
We belong to a global community and our children are becoming "global kids." Comparing and understanding different languages and cultures is more vital than ever! Additionally, learning a foreign language reinforces a child's overall education. Early childhood is the optimal time for children to learn a second language, and the Teach Me Everyday language series is a practical and inspiring way to teach them. Through story and song, each book and audio encourages them to listen, speak, read and write in a foreign language.

Today's "global kids" hold tomorrow's world in their hands. So when it comes to learning a new language, don't be surprised when they say, "teach me!"

The Hebrew language uses a different alphabet than English, often called the Alef-Bet. Hebrew is also written and read from right to left, as opposed to English from left to right. The Alef-Bet consists of 27 characters and has no vowels. Vowel markings, called nikkud, can be added to each character to identify the vowel sound associated with the word. The process of transliteration is used to write Hebrew words using the Roman or the English alphabet. There are many different ways to transliterate words, so the spellings may vary widely based on phonetics and style. There is no right or wrong transliteration as each version has a valid spelling.

Teach Me Everyday Hebrew
Volume One
ISBN 13: 978-1-59972-105-7
Library of Congress PCN: 2008902662

Copyright © 2008 by Teach Me Tapes, Inc.
6016 Blue Circle Drive, Minnetonka, MN 55343
www.teachmetapes.com

Book Design by Design Lab, Northfield, MN

INDEX & SONG LIST

Ksheh Anachnu Beyachad (The More We Get Together) **page 4**

Tzipor Ktana (Little Bird) **page 9**

Achinu Yaakov? (Are You Sleeping?) **page 9**

Yemay Hashavuah (Days of the Week) **page 11**

Rosh, Ktefayim, Birkayim, Etzba'ot (Head, Shoulders, Knees and Toes) **page 12**

Geshem (Rain Medley) **page 15**

Hamisparim (The Numbers) **page 17**

Alef-Bet (Alphabet Song) **page 17**

Gdi Katan Haya le Miri (Mary Had a Little Lamb) **page 18**

Pilon Echad (One Elephant) **page 19**

Geshem, Geshem (Rain, Rain) **page 20**

Kulam Mocha'im Iti Kaf (Everyone Clap Hands With Me) **page 20**

Galgalay Ha Mechonit (The Wheels on the Car) **page 21**

Numi Itzmi (Hush Little Baby) **page 22**

Al Hagesher (On the Bridge of Avignon) **page 23**

Nad Ned (Swing) **page 24**

Hashafan Hakatan (Little Rabbit) **page 25**

Shisha Barvazim (Six Little Ducks) **page 25**

Oh! Susanna (Oh! Susanna) **page 27**

Me'ir Me'ir Kochav Katan (Twinkle, Twinkle Little Star) **page 28**

Numi, Numi (Sleep, Sleep) **page 28**

Laila Tov Yedidai (Goodnight My Friends) **page 29**

Ksheh Anachnu Beyachad

Ksheh anachnu beyachad, beyachad, beyachad
Ksheh anachnu beyachad, kulanu smechim
Yedidai hem yedidecha
Yedidecha hem yedidai
Ksheh anachnu beyachad, kulanu smechim.

The More We Get Together

The more we get together, together, together
The more we get together the happier we'll be
For your friends are my friends
And my friends are your friends
The more we get together the happier we'll be.

♪ **כשאנחנו ביחד**

כשאנחנו ביחד ביחד ביחד
כשאנחנו ביחד כלנו שמחים
ידידי הם ידידיך
ידידיך הם ידידי
כשאנחנו ביחד כלנו שמחים.

זו החתולה שלי.
הוראים לה מיצי.
צבעה אפור.

Zo hachatoola sheli.
Korim la Mitzi.
Tziv'a afor.

My cat.
Her name is Mitzi.
She is gray.

זה החתול שלי

זה הכלב שלי.
קוראים לו מוקי.

Zeh hakelev sheli.
Korim lo Muki.

My dog.
His name is Muki.

זה הכלב שלי

זֶה הַבַּיִת שֶׁלִי.
גַּגוֹ אָדוֹם, וּבַגִּינָה
פְּרָחִים צְהֻבִּים פּוֹרְחִים.

Zeh habayit sheli.
Gago adom, uvaginah prachim
tzehoobim porchim.

This is my house.
It has a red roof and a garden
with yellow flowers.

שְׁמוֹנֶה
Shmoneh

8

צבע חדרי הוא כחול.
השעה שבע.
הגיע זמן להתעורר!
הגיע זמן להתעורר!

Tzeva chadri hu kachol.
Hasha'a shevah.
Higi'a zman l'hitorer!
Higi'a zman l'hitorer!

My room is blue.
It is seven o'clock.
Time to get up!
Time to get up!

Tzipor Ktana
Tzipor ktana, tzipor nechmada
Tzipor yafa, ani ohevet otach
Ani rotza la'oof itach
Ani rotza la'oof itach
La'oof itach, la'oof itach.

Little Bird
Little bird, lovely bird
Beautiful bird, I love you
I would like to fly with you
I would like to fly with you
Fly with you, fly with you.

צ♪פ♫ר קטנה
ציפור קטנה, ציפור נחמדה
ציפור יפה, אני אוהבת אותך
אני רוצה לעוף איתך
אני רוצה לעוף איתך
לעוף איתך, לעוף איתך.

Achinu Yaakov?
Achinu Yaakov, achinu Yaakov?
Al tishan, al tishan
Ha pa'amon metzaltzel
Ha pa'amon metzaltzel
Ding dang dong! Ding dang dong!

Are You Sleeping?
Are you sleeping, are you sleeping?
Brother John, Brother John
Morning bells are ringing
Morning bells are ringing
Ding dang dong! Ding dang dong!

אחינו יעקב?
אחינו יעקב, אחינו יעקב?
אל תישן, אל תישן
הפעמון מצלצל
הפעמון מצלצל
דינג דנג דונג! דינג דנג דונג!

Hayom yom rishon.
Ha'im ata yode'a et yemay hashavuah?

Today is Sunday.
Do you know the days of the week?

עֶשֶׂר
Eser

יום ראשון

Yom Rishon
Sunday

יום שני

Yom Sheni
Monday

יום שלישי

Yom Shlishi
Tuesday

יום רביעי

Yom Revi'i
Wednesday

יום חמישי

Yom Chamishi
Thursday

יום שישי

Yom Shishi
Friday

יום שבת

Yom Shabat
Saturday

אחת עשרה
Achat esreh

11

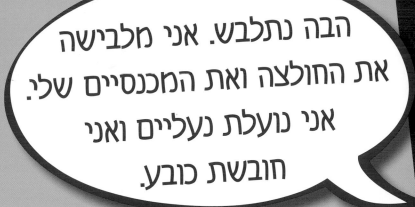

Hava nitlabesh.
Ani malbisha et hachultzah
ve'et hamichnasayim sheli. Ani noelet
naalayim ve´ani choveshet kova.

Let's get dressed.
I put on my shirt
and pants. I put on my shoes
and my hat.

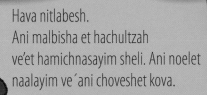

ראש, כתפיים, ברכיים, אצבעות

ראש, כתפיים, ברכיים, אצבעות
ראש, כתפיים, ברכיים, אצבעות
עיניים, אוזניים, פה ואף
ראש, כתפיים, ברכיים, אצבעות.

Rosh, Ktefayim, Birkayim, Etzba'ot
Rosh, ktefayim, birkayim, etzba'ot
Rosh, ktefayim, birkayim, etzba'ot
Aynayim, oznayim, peh, v'af
Rosh, ktefayim, birkayim, etzba'ot.

Head, Shoulders, Knees and Toes
Head, shoulders, knees and toes, knees and toes
Head, shoulders, knees and toes, knees and toes
Eyes and ears and mouth and nose
Head, shoulders, knees and toes, knees and toes.

לארוחת בוקר אני אוכלת לחם עם ריבה ושותה שוקו חם.

Le'aruchat boker
ani ochelet lechem
im reba vi shotah shoko cham.

For breakfast
I eat bread and jelly
with hot chocolate.

יורד גשם בחוץ.
איני יכול לצאת החוצה היום.

Yored geshem bachutz.
Eini yachol latzet hachutza hayom.

It is raining outside.
I cannot go outside today.

Geshem

Geshem, geshem higamer
Vetachzor beyom acher
Geshem, geshem higamer
Vetachzor beyom acher.

Lifamim kchulim, lifamim yerookim
Hatzva'im hachi yafim sheh ra'iti ba chayim
Vroodim, sgoolim, tzehoobim - whi!
Ani ohevet lirot et ha keshet.

Rain Medley

Rain, rain, go away
Come again another day
Rain, rain, go away
Little Johnny wants to play.

It's raining, it's pouring
The old man is snoring
He bumped his head and went to bed
And couldn't get up in the morning.

Sometimes blue and sometimes green
Prettiest colors I've ever seen
Pink and purple, yellow - whee!
I love to ride those rainbows.

גשם

גשם, גשם היגמר
ותחזור ביום אחר
גשם, גשם היגמר
ותחזור ביום אחר.

לפעמים כחולים, לפעמים ירוקים
הצבעים הכי יפים שראיתי בחיים
ורודים, סגולים, צהובים- ווי!
אני אוהבת לראות את הקשת.

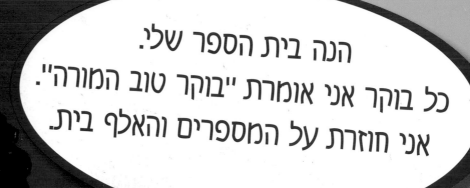

הנה בית הספר שלי.
כל בוקר אני אומרת "בוקר טוב המורה".
אני חוזרת על המספרים והאלף בית.

Henay bet hasafer sheli.
Kol boker ani omeret "Boker tov, hamorah."
Ani chozeret al hamisparim v'ha'alef-bet.

Here is my school.
I say, "Good morning, teacher."
I repeat the numbers and alphabet.

בית הספר שלי

מספרים

10	9	8	7	6	5	4	3	2	1
עשר	תשע	שמונה	שבע	שש	חמש	ארבע	שלש	שתים	אחת

Numbers

achat	shtaim	shalosh	arba	chamesh	shesh	sheva	shmoneh	tesha	eser
one	two	three	four	five	six	seven	eight	nine	ten

אלף בית

א Alef (Silent)	ב Bet (B/V)	ג Gimel (G)	ד Dalet (D)	ה He (H)	ו Vav (V/O/U)	ז Zayin (Z)	ח Chet (Ch)	ט Tet (T)
י Yod (Y)	כ Kaf (K/CH)	ך Final Kaf (CH)	ל Lamed (L)	ם Final Mem (M)	מ Mem (M)	ן Final Nun (N)	נ Nun (N)	ס Samekh (S)
ע Ayin (Silent)	ף Final Fe (F)	פ Pe/Fe (P/F)	ץ Tzadi Final (TZ)	צ Tzadi (TZ)	ק Qoph (Q)	ר Resh (R)	ש Shin (Sh)	ת Tav (silent T)

אלף בית
א,ב,אב
גדה,גדה
וזח,וזח
טיכ,טיכ
למנ,למנ
סעפ,סעפ
צקר,צקר
ש ו-ת, ש ו-ת

Alef-Bet Song
Alef-Bet, Alef-Bet
Gimel Dalet Hay, Gimel Dalet Hay
Vav Zayin Chet, Vav Zayin Chet
Tet Yud Kaf, Tet Yud Kaf
Lamed Mem Noon, Lamed Mem Noon
Samech Ayin Pay, Samech Ayin Pay
Tzadi Koof Raish, Tzadi Koof Raish
Shin v'Tav, Shin v'Tav.

*Note: The Hebrew Alef Bet consists of 27 characters and has no vowels. It is written and read from right to left. Transliteration is the process of using Roman letters to write out Hebrew words, but is written and read the opposite of the Hebrew letters, from left to right.

שבע עשרה
Shva esreh

גדי קטן היה למירי

גדי קטן היה למירי, היה למירי, היה למירי
גדי קטן היה למירי, גדי לבן וצח
ולכל מקום שהיא הלכה, היא הלכה, היא הלכה
ולכל מקום שהיא הלכה, הגדי איתה הלך.

Gdi Katan Haya le Miri

Gdi katan haya le Miri, haya le Miri, haya le Miri
Gdi katan haya le Miri, gdi lavan v'tzach
Uleh chol makom sheh hi halcha, hi halcha, hi halcha
Uleh chol makom sheh hi halcha, ha gdi ita halach.

Mary Had a Little Lamb

Mary had a little lamb, little lamb, little lamb
Mary had a little lamb, its fleece was white as snow
Everywhere that Mary went, Mary went, Mary went
Everywhere that Mary went, the lamb was sure to go.

שמונה עשרה
Shmoneh esreh

פילון אחד

שני פילונים יצאו לשחק
יום אחד על קורה עכביש
הם נהנו מאד מאד
ויקראו לעוד פילון לבוא.

שלושה פילונים יצאו לשחק...
ארבעה פילונים יצאו לשחק...
כל הפילונים יצאו לשחק...

Pilon Echad
Shnei pilonim yatzoo lesachek
Yom echad al koreh akavish
Hem nehenoo me'od me'od
V'karoo leh od pilon lavo.

Shlosha pilonim yatzoo lesachek...
Arba'a pilonim yatzoo lesachek...
Kol hapilonim yatzoo lesachek...

One Elephant
One elephant went out to play
Upon a spider's web one day
He had such enormous fun that
He called for another elephant to come.

Two elephants went out to play...
Three elephants went out to play...
All the elephants went out to play...

גשם גשם

גשם גשם משמים
כל היום טיפות המים
טיף טף, טיף טף
מחאו, כף אל כף
טיף טף, טיף טף
טיף טיף טף, טיף טיף טף
מחאו כף אל כף.

Geshem, Geshem

Geshem, geshem, mi shamayim
Kol hayom tipot hamayim
Tif tif taf, tif tif taf
Macha'oo, kaf el kaf
Tif taf, tif taf
Tif tif taf, tif tif taf
Macha'oo, kaf el kaf.

Rain, Rain

Rain, rain, from the sky
Rain drops all day long
Tif tif taf, tif tif taf
Tip tap, let's clap
Tif taf, tif taf
Tif tif taf, tif tif taf
Tip tap, let's clap.

כלם מוחאים איתי כף

כלם מוחאים איתי כף (מחיאת כף)
כלם מוחאים איתי כף (מחיאת כף)
אולי תצטרפי למשחה (מחיאת כף)
כלם מוחאים איתי כף (מחיאת כף)

כולם מנסים כאן לשרוק... (שריקה)
כולם רוקעים ברגליים... (רקיעות)
כולם מקישים אצבעות... (הקשה)

Kulam Mocha'im Iti Kaf

Kulam mocha'im iti kaf! (clap, clap)
Kulam mocha'im iti kaf! (clap, clap)
Oolai titztarfoo lamischak? (clap, clap)
Kulam mocha'im iti kaf! (clap, clap)

Kulam menasim kan lishrok...(whistle)
Kulam rok'im baraglayim...(stamp, stamp)
Kulam makishim etzba'ot...(snap, snap)

Everyone Clap Hands With Me

Everyone clap hands with me!
Everyone clap hands with me!
Will you join our game?
Everyone clap hands with me!

Everyone try to whistle with me...
Everyone stamp feet with me...
Everyone snap fingers with me...

אחרי בית הספר אנחנו הולכים הביתה.

Acharay bet hasefer,
anachnu holchim habaitah.

After school,
we go home.

Galgalay Ha Mechonit

Galgalay ha mechonit mistovevim
Mistovevim, mistovevim
Galgalay ha mechonit mistovevim
Ben rechovot ha ir.

Ha tzaftzefa taoferet bip bip
Tzoferet bip bip, tzoferet bip bip
Ha tzaftzefa tzoferet bip bip
Ben rechovot ha ir.

Ha yeladim korim, "hegeah zman le'echol"
"Zman le'echol, zman le'echol"
Ha yeladim korim, "hegeah zman le'echol"
Ben rechovot ha ir.

The Wheels on the Car
The wheels on the car go round and round
Round and round, round and round
The wheels on the car go round and round
All around the town.

The horn on the car goes beep beep beep
Beep beep beep, beep beep beep
The horn on the car goes beep beep beep
All around the town.

The children in the car go, "Let's have lunch"
"Let's have lunch, let's have lunch"
The children in the car go, "Let's have lunch"
All around the town.

גלגלי המכונית

גלגלי המכונית מסתובבים
מסתובבים, מסתובבים
גלגלי המכונית מסתובבים
בין רחובות העיר.

הצפצפה צופרת ביפ ביפ
צופרת ביפ ביפ, צופרת ביפ ביפ
הצפצפה צופרת ביפ ביפ
בין רחובות העיר.

הילדים קוראים "הגיע הזמן לאכול"
"זמן לאכול, זמן לאכול"
הילדים קוראים "הגיע הזמן לאכול"
בין רחובות העיר.

עשרים ואחת
Esrim ve'achat

21

אוכלים ארוחת צהריים.
אחרי הארוחה,
אנחנו נחים.

Ochlim aruchat tzohorayim.
Acharay ha arucha,
anachnu nachim.

It's lunch time.
After lunch,
we take a nap.

Numi Itzmi
Numi itzmi et eynayich yalda
Abba yikneh lach tzipor nechmadah
V'im hatzipor te'alem bimoofah
Abba yikneh lach taba'at yaffa
V'im ha taba'at tovad at tir'i
Abba yikneh lach masrek oore'i
V'im hare'i lirsisim yitnapetz
Abba yikneh od echad bishvilech.

נומי עצמי
נומי עצמי את עינייך ילדה
אבא יקנה לך ציפור נחמדה
ואם הציפור תיעלם במעופה
אבא יקנה לך טבעת יפה
ואם הטבעת תאבד את תראי
אבא יקנה לך מסרק וראי
ואם הראי לרסיסים יתנפץ
אבא יקנה עוד אחד בשבילך.

Hush Little Baby
Hush little baby don't say a word
Papa's going to buy you a mockingbird
If that mockingbird won't sing
Papa's going to buy you a diamond ring
If that diamond ring turns brass
Papa's going to buy you a looking glass
If that looking glass falls down
You'll still be the sweetest little baby in town.

עשרים ושתיים
Esrim ushtaim

22

Acharay menuchat tzohorayim nelech la park.
Ani roah et ha barvazim. Ani shara ve rokedet
im yedidai al ha gesher.

After our naps we go to the park.
I see the ducks. I sing and dance
with my friends on the bridge.

אחרי מנוחת צהריים
נלך לפארק. אני רואה את
הברווזים. אני שרה ורוקדת עם
ידידיי על הגשר.

Al Hagesher
Al hagesher, al hagesher
Kulam rokdim, kulam rokdim
Al hagesher, al hagesher
Kulam rokdim ba ma'agal.

On the Bridge of Avignon
On the bridge of Avignon
They're all dancing, they're all dancing
On the bridge of Avignon
They're all dancing round and round.

על הגשר
על הגשה, על הגשר
כולם רוקדים, כולם רוקדים
על הגשה, על הגשר
כולם רוקדים במעגל.

נד נד

נד נד, נד נד, רד עלה, עלה ורד
נד נד, נד נד, רד עלה, עלה ורד
מי למעלה? מי למטה? רק אני, אני ואתה!
נד נד, נד נד, רד עלה, עלה ורד.

Nad Ned

Nad ned, nad ned, red aleh, aleh va red
Nad ned, nad ned, red aleh, aleh va red
Mi limalah? Mi lamata? Rak ani, ani vi ata!
Nad ned, nad ned, red aleh, aleh va red.

Swing

Swing, swing, up and down
Swing, swing, up and down
Who's up? Who's down? Only me and you!
Swing, swing, up and down.

Hashafan Hakatan

Hashafan, hakatan shachach lisgor hadelet
Hitztanen hamisken ve kibel nazelet
La la la apchi, la la la apchi
La la la apchi, la la la la.

השפן הקטן

♪

השפן הקטן שכח לסגור הדלת
הצטנן המסכן וקבל נזלת
לה לה לה אפצ'י, לה לה לה אפצ'י
לה לה לה אפצ'י, לה לה לה לה.

Little Rabbit

The little rabbit forgot to close the door
He was chilled and caught a cold
La la la achoo, la la la achoo
La la la achoo, la la la la.

Shisha Barvazim

Shisha barvazim
Sheh hikarti pa'am
Shamen ve razeh ve yafeh gam
Aval ha katan im notza al gabo
Hovil et kulam im
Ha "ga" shello
Ha "ga" shello
Ha "ga" shello.
Hovil et kulam im
Ha "ga" shello.

שישה ברווזים

♪ ♫

שישה ברווזים
שהיכרתי פעם
שמן ורזה ויפה גם
אבל הקטן עם נוצה על גבו
הוביל את כולם עם
ה"גה" שלו
ה"גה" שלו
ה"גה" שלו.
הוביל את כולם עם
ה"גה" שלו.

Six Little Ducks

Six little ducks that I once knew
Fat ones, skinny ones, fair ones too
But the one little duck
With the feather on his back
He led the others with his
Quack, quack, quack
Quack, quack, quack
Quack, quack, quack.
He led the others with his
Quack, quack, quack.

אֲנִי רְעֵבָה! הִגִּיעַ הַזְּמַן לֶאֱכוֹל אֲרוּחַת עֶרֶב.

Ani re'eva!
Higi'a z'man le'echol aruchat erev.

I am hungry!
It is dinner time.

Oh! Susanna

Bati mi Alabama im ha banjo al birki
Ani holech le Louisiana kday lirrot et ahoovati
Oh! Susanna, al tivki bishvili
Ki bati mi Alabama im ha banjo al birki.

Oh! Susanna

Well, I come from Alabama with my banjo on my knee
I'm goin' to Louisiana, my true love for to see
Oh! Susanna, won't you cry for me
'Cause I come from Alabama with my banjo on my knee.

או! סוזנה

באתי מאלבמה עם הבנג'ו על ברכי
אני הולך ללואיזיאנה כדי לראות את אהובתי
או! סוזנה אל תבכי בשבילי
כי באתי מאלבמה עם הבנג'ו על ברכי.

עשרים ושבע
Esrim vesheva

הגיע לילה.
האם אתה יכול לראות את
הכוכבים בשמים?

Higi'a lailah.
Ha'im ata yachol lirot et
hakochavim bashamayim?

It's night time.
Do you see
the stars?

מאיר מאיר כוכב קטן

מאיר מאיר כוכב קטן
אינני יודע מי אתה
כוכב רחוק כוכב גבוה
כמו יהלום בשמים
מאיר מאיר כוכב קטן
אינני יודע מי אתה.

Me'ir Me'ir Kochav Katan

Me'ir me'ir kochav katan
Ayneni yodeah mi ata
Kochav rachok kochav gavoah
Kmo yahalom bashamayim
Me'ir me'ir kochav katan
Ayneni yodeah mi ata.

Twinkle, Twinkle Little Star

Twinkle, twinkle, little star
How I wonder what you are
Up above the world so high
Like a diamond in the sky
Twinkle, twinkle, little star
How I wonder what you are.

נומי נומי

נומי נומי ילדתי
נומי נומי לי
נומי נומי ילדתי
נומי נומי לי.

אבא הלך לעבודה
הלך הלך אבא
ישוב עם צאת הלבנה
יביא לך מתנה.

Numi, Numi

Numi, numi yaldati
Numi, numi li
Numi, numi yaldati
Numi, numi li.

Abba halach la'avodah
Halach, halach abba
Yashoov im tzet halevana
Yavi lach matanah.

Sleep, Sleep

Sleep, sleep, my little child
Sleep, sleep child
Sleep, sleep, my little child
Sleep, sleep child.

Daddy went to work
He went, Daddy went
He'll return when the moon comes out
He'll bring you a present.

עשרים ושמונה
Esrim veshmonch

28

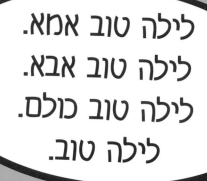

Laila tov, ima.
Laila tov, abba.
Laila tov, kulam.
Laila tov.

Goodnight, Mommy.
Goodnight, Daddy.
Goodnight, everyone.
Goodnight.

לילה טוב
לילה טוב ידידי, לילה טוב
לילה טוב ידידי, לילה טוב
לילה טוב ידידי
לילה טוב ידידי
לילה טוב ידידי, לילה טוב
להתראות

Laila Tov Yedidai
Laila tov yedidai, laila tov
Laila tov yedidai, laila tov
Laila tov yedidai
Laila tov yedidai
Laila tov yedidai, laila tov
L'hitra'ot!

Goodnight My Friends
Goodnight my friends, goodnight
Goodnight my friends, goodnight
Goodnight my friends
Goodnight my friends
Goodnight my friends, goodnight
Goodnight!

רוצים ללמוד עוד?
(Want to learn more?)

מנורה
menorah
lamp

בנג'ו
banjo
banjo

ספה
sapah
couch

כדור
kadur
ball

כלב
kelev, dog

כרית
karit
pillow

חלון
chalon
window

מיטה
mita
bed

בובה
buba
doll

שלושים
Shloshim

30

שוקו חם

shoko cham
hot cocoa

מיץ תפוזים

mitz tapuzim
orange juice

לחם

ריבה

riba
jam

lechem, bread

עץ

etz
tree

ידיד

yedid
friend

גשר

gesher
bridge

כדורגל

kaduregel
soccer ball

שלושים ואחת
Shloshim ve'echad

31

צבעים

אדום
adom
red

סגול
sagol
purple

כחול
kachol
blue

כתום
katom
orange

ירוק
yarok
green

צהוב
tzahov
yellow

אפור
afor
gray

חום
chum
brown

ורוד
varod
pink

שחור
shachor
black

לבן
lavan
white